The Timing *of* Everything PROMISED
From Despair to Resilience

Faith Journey Publishing

The Timing of Everything PROMISED
From Despair to Resilience

Published 2024
Printed in the United States of America
ISBN: 979-8-9858168-8-4

Compiled and edited by Mari Fitz-Wynn
Publications Coordinator: Kimball Honoré McNeal
Artwork by Nicki Black
Cover design by Leah Morrison

For information, contact:
Faith Journey Publishing, LLC
contact@faithjourneypublishing.com

Contents

FOREWORD

Resilience.

The power of resilience echoes through each of the following stories.

When faith follows despair, each woman reaches deep into her soul to find an unknown strength to press on.

Disaster. Despair. An exodus. A time of lament. A time of mourning and complaining. Through this pattern of faith, resilience is formed.

The introductory story of Ruth sets the tone for this pattern when Naomi returns to her homeland after devastating loss. When she first sets foot back home, Naomi greets her old acquaintances with grief and bitterness. Yet the more time she spends rooted in the traditions and faith of her homeland, the more the ways of her people give her a foundation to settle and recenter.

Somehow,

after a period of mourning.

she rises up

is able to assess her situation.

And is able to discern clearly what practical steps to take next.

In returning home, after a period of grief, she receives a sudden clarity on what steps to take next.

In the following stories, clarity arises after calamity in a similar way.

A pattern of gaining awareness of a situation, grieving a loss, mourning the loss, searching for a solution, and gathering strength to carry on weaves through each story.

A combination of faith, traditions, and familiar teaching intertwine from threads into a rope of strength that can pull a woman up through setbacks. After a period of mourning, grieving, and lamenting a loss, a voice deep down in her soul guides a woman to pick up, stand, take steps and move forward.

This anthology of stories reflect the resilience to carry on in difficult and despairing situations that life presents. In each story, these women uncover a core strength that allows them to press on despite heartbreaking circumstances. Each woman comes through a period of questioning themselves and God. Each woman experiences the pain of decisions made by loved ones that affect their lives.

Somehow, despite anguish and affliction, each woman receives the clarity, peace and strength to carry forward and take a step forward, out of the pit.

God's faithfulness endures through each story.
God's faithfulness endures in our own lives.

Somehow, He makes a way to give beauty for ashes and the oil of joy for mourning when we return home to Him.

When we find the presence to wait on Him, and Him alone.

I waited patiently for the Lord.
He inclined to me and heard my cry.
He drew me up from the pit of destruction,
Out of the miry bog,
And set my feet upon a rock,
Making my steps secure.
He put a new song in my mouth,
A song of praise to our God.
Many will see and fear,
And put their trust in the Lord.
Psalm 40:1-2 (ESV)

It is our hope as you read these stories you will be encouraged by the thread of hope woven through each one, hope that comes from the Lord who rescues us from the pit of destruction and sets our feet upon a rock to stand.

And as women who stand after a time of despair, may we hold each other up with words of encouragement and songs of praise to the God who delivers us. Through our words and songs may others see and put their trust in the Lord.

My source of resilience roots in the strength of my mother, who left her mother's side to journey across the Pacific Ocean from the Philippines to begin a new life with a man she barely knew. Her life in America became a place of nurturing and compassion for others who began anew in a new land with new language, food and customs. She loved Jesus with her whole heart and displayed His countenance of mercy and peace through the nine decades of her life, even as the last ten were tainted with the disease of Alzheimer's. It was my honor to care for her in my home the last decade of her life, and to witness the Weight of Glory in her room the last hours of her life, a confirmation that even in death God's glory shines. Our favorite song to sing together those last years was "O Ilaw," which means O Light in Tagalog, the language of her country.

There is a verse in this song that says

Oh, light in the cold night
Oh, ilaw sa gabing malamig
You are like a star in the sky
Wangis mo'y bituin sa langit

Oh, torch in the silent night
Oh, tanglaw sa gabing tahimik

Your picture, Mother, caused pain
Larawan mo, Neneng, nagbigay-pasakit

The pain of witnessing her deteriorating mind and body was overshadowed by the light of her love and tenderness even to her last breath.

Love and faith breed resilience. A resilience that endures to our last breath. ~ Vina Mogg

INTRODUCTION

Times had grown bad, life in their community seemed worse than ever, and try as they might, their efforts to remain were not working out. Constantly grappling with insurmountable challenges, relocation appeared to be the only viable solution. The harsh realities of their situation left them with no choice. Today was the day they would pack up and go. Destitute and driven to despair, she realized the decision was not hard.

As Ruth readied herself to say goodbye to their home of ten years, the difficulty of it all was overwhelming. So, with hearts heavy and spirits worn, they started the move; but before long, things took another turn for the worse. The plan had changed, and she would not continue the trip. But the young woman would not be thwarted and clung to her friend, the woman who had supported and helped her through her darkest days — her mother-in-law, Naomi.

She persisted, insisting that she could not, she must not, leave Naomi's side. We read of Ruth's great love, commitment, hope, and trust for Naomi, refusing to let desperate circumstances separate them. Ruth is willing to forsake her gods for Naomi's One True God and become her Israelite daughter to continue to share life with her. In the Book of Ruth, we read how God brought Ruth from despair to resilience, rescuing her from a seemingly impossible situation and raising her to prominence in His Divine Plan.

"'But Ruth replied, 'Don't urge me to leave you or to turn back from you. Where you go, I will go, and where you stay, I will stay. Your people will be my people and your God my God,'" embodying a profound loyalty that pushes past her despair. (Ruth 1:16-17 CSV).

What propels one person towards resilience while others falter in the face of adversity and despair? What inner force prevents us from succumbing to hopelessness and abandoning our faith? No simple formula exists for this question, yet the apostle Paul provides a glimpse into its essence in Hebrews 6:19, where he speaks of an "anchor of the soul" — a stabilizing force. Much like a ship's anchor ensures its safety and stability in turbulent waters, our metaphorical anchor must be steadfast and reliable to guide us through life's storms.

In times of trial, Christ, our anchor, holds us steadfast; devoted to loved ones, to faith, to purpose, He alone steadies the soul and provides the strength to persevere. Just as Ruth found refuge in her unwavering commitment to Naomi, we too can find solace and resilience in holding firm to our faith in God against the tempests of life. In the story of Ruth and Naomi, we find scriptures reflecting human resilience, a timeless testament to the enduring power of faith and love. It is a narrative that resonates across the ages, reminding us that even in our darkest hour, we are never alone. Just as Ruth stood by Naomi's side, so too does our Savior guide us through the trials of this world to ensure that we experience His faithful promises.

Despair is characterized by a sense of hopelessness, powerlessness, and overwhelming sadness in the face of adversity or challenging circumstances. Despair can leave us feeling like we are trapped in a dark tunnel with no light at the end.

Resilience, on the other hand, is our ability to bounce back from setbacks, adapt, and thrive despite difficult circumstances. With resilience, when we experience hardship or struggle, we find the strength and courage to persevere. Resilience empowers us to face challenges head-on, to learn and grow from our experiences, and to emerge stronger and more capable than before.

Moving from despair to resilience is a transformative journey that often involves a shift in perspective. It includes seeking support from loved ones, finding meaning and purpose in our experiences, cultivating a sense of hope and optimism for the future, and ultimately, trusting in the faithfulness and promises of God in our darkest moments. Our trust in God gives us the power to overcome and thrive.

Our deliverance from despair rests on the incomprehensible love of God, who did not spare His Son and rescued us by the work of the cross. We are assured that His will and His plan will be carried out in our lives. His love gives us victory. By faith we are and will be resilient.

Each story included in this anthology encapsulates a profound truth about the human experience, particularly that of women. The following stories touch on the universal theme of finding hope and resilience in the face of despair.

We hope to not only provide a platform for women to express their experiences, but also offer a source of inspiration and comfort to uplift and empower others who may be facing similar challenges. Often through shared struggles and vulnerabilities, and through faith in God, we find the greatest strength and resilience within ourselves. Finding this strength speaks to the innate human desire to overcome adversity with courage, determination, with the One who will never leave our side.

I have no doubt this anthology will touch the hearts of women everywhere, reminding them that they are not alone in their struggles and that hope can always be found, even in the darkest of times. We become resilient through God alone, even when we are unaware of the resilience in us.

~ Mari Fitz-Wynn

Restored: The Story of God's Faithfulness

To explain how I became a Christian, let me first emphasize the importance of recognizing the power of the gospel to save an entire household. When my younger brother, Jason, was born with Down's Syndrome, my father, a widely successful man, became deeply depressed because he did not know how to respond to the greatest trial of his life. To save my father, a local Chinese Christian church began to share the gospel with our family—patiently and yet persistently.

Through the work of the Holy Spirit and the love of these disciples, my parents experienced rich spiritual transformation and came to believe in Christ as their savior. My parents, immigrants from Taiwan, were the first in all generations to know Jesus. Subsequently, in the last 25 years, I have witnessed my grandparents coming to Christ, physically destroying idols in their house and replacing the former altars in their home with the words of God: "...But as for me and my house, we will serve the Lord." (Joshua 24:15 ESV). Because of this transformation, I was raised in a Christian household, and I saw, from an early age, that my parents loved and believed in a true and living God. Therefore, my belief in God came through experiencing my parents living out their faith—a historicized and powerful demonstration of God's sovereignty to save a new generation.

My family had the most significant influence on my spiritual growth. I grew up watching and learning from my parents' spiritual journey in coming to know Christ. As a family, we dedicated our time and energy to developing an inclusive community of youth leaders, and it was through this community that I first learned about what it means to share everything we had. At the same time, my brother's disability became an immense blessing to my family and the church community.

As his sister, I learned to navigate patience and compassion—and am still learning to do so. Like the blind man who was healed in John 9, I saw that my brother's disability happened so "that the works of God might be displayed in him" (John 9:3 ESV). My parents started a Special Needs Ministry at that local church, and the ministry drew dozens of families to the gospel—and for 15 years, they co-taught an "adults with disabilities" class every Sunday.

At the end of high school, I felt a calling to go into education. I began to develop a strong passion as a student representative for the district's Board of Education and became involved in many educational endeavors. When letters of college acceptance came, I chose to go to the state university of New Jersey—Rutgers University— to pursue education.

My time at Rutgers was a smattering of worldly success. I became heavily involved in college life, serving as the president of the program association and managing half a million dollars. I graduated at the top of my class in three years and received my master's degree in education in my fourth year —becoming the graduate school's commencement speaker. I received two job offers in one day before spring break and was selected as one of the top 18 leaders in the university. College life proved to be easy and fulfilling, but I began to see my achievements as my own doing.

However, near the end of my successful college career, life took an unexpected turn. One summer, I signed up to go on a short-term mission trip abroad with my local Chinese Christian church. I was excited and eager to see how God would develop my heart for missions. Since the mission trip abroad was to a rural area, we were required to take a physical examination and blood test before leaving. To my surprise, my routine blood tests showed abnormal liver enzymes. My doctor was alarmed, and called, and forbade me to go on the trip until he was able to diagnose the problem. After many rounds of testing, I was diagnosed with Primary Sclerosing Cholangitis (PSC), a rare biliary liver disease that affects only 1 in 10,000 people. In addition, I was a young Asian female, a very rare occurrence. There is no cure for PSC, and I was told that my life quality would deteriorate. The only cure was a liver transplant, which I needed within the next 10-20 years. At age 21, I learned that I had a terminal disease, one that could only be cured by the transplant. Without a transplant, I would get sicker and sicker each year.

After graduation, before starting my new job as a high school English teacher, I took the summer to work for International Justice Mission, a Christian human rights agency that works to rescue victims of violent oppression. In those three months, with my new diagnosis, my worldview was incredibly changed. I began to see the world from a greater perspective, seeing myself and my worldly accomplishments as prideful and insignificant in relation to what God had planned for His people. My heart was uprooted, and I saw the mortality of my sin—I had thought that being a Christian meant only living a moral and excellent life, but in fact, I had only been obedient to my own path. Becoming a disciple meant pursuing justice, righteousness, and ultimately suffering for the Lord. My life took a complete 180 degree turn, and I began to wake up—turning my heart of stone into a heart of flesh for the Lord. I started my teaching career as a high school English teacher and became deeply rooted in understanding and working against social inequities with my students.

This burning desire for making social change did not disappear. After three years of an amazing teaching experience, I decided to leave its comforts and pursue a doctoral degree. I chose to attend Columbia University and move to New York City. I intended to start fresh; I was 25, accepted into a top program, single, and going to live with one of my best friends: "Hello, New York City!" I began to feel that life was easy once again. Yet three days before my move, I was hospitalized due to PSC. Little did I know that this was only the first of six hospitalizations during a difficult and intense year. I went through a trying amount of emergency procedures—each time was a life-threatening situation. It seemed unreal. I spent my weeks studying, writing papers, going to the hospital, and trying to find community despite the limited mental and physical energy I had. I questioned God's provision. During my fourth hospital stay, I realized my identity was not defined by a new place, but by Christ alone. In my weakest moment, after I had pleaded to the Lord to take the suffering away three times, I was reminded of 2 Corinthians 12:8-10 (ESV): "Three times, I pleaded with the Lord...But he said to me, 'My grace is sufficient for you, for my power is made perfect in weakness...'" I told the Lord that all the boasting in my work counted as nothing compared to knowing Him. He humbled me and taught me that His grace was immeasurable. Only through Christ's power could I experience immense joy. I never understood what Paul meant, until that night, and from then on, I began to respond with joy—joy that completely sustains.

Yet responding with joy was not easy. The hospitalizations continued. The cycles of illness happened many times in graduate school; I wondered if I could possibly pursue a career, let alone a marriage or a fulfilling life. Along with the physical suffering, I experienced two heartbreaks in my twenty's because of my illness. In the first heartbreak, my beloved's family could not accept me because they did not want their son to marry an unhealthy woman. In the second heartbreak, the man ended the relationship after seeing me hospitalized, stating that he did not want a life of hardship and marrying me would promise that. I was rejected twice because of my illness. I could not release the idea that I was rejected for being who I was. I began to doubt the way I was made in God's image and started a spiral of self-rejection.

I was attending Redeemer Presbyterian Church in New York City during this time. I joined the Gotham Fellowship in 2014-2015, a fellowship program for young professionals to explore the intersection of faith and work. During the closing reflection session at the winter retreat for this fellowship I wrote a letter to God, and asked a question: if He indeed was a healer, would He heal me from my disease? At the time, I had little faith and a lot of doubt on whether that would be true. I was significantly chronically ill, and technically unemployed as a doctoral student—anxious and uncertain about my future. In fact, I had to Skype into the winter retreat because I had another episode of acute illness and was unable to physically attend. At that time, I also prayed that God would show me how to still live my life with purpose with my illness and to redeem and restore me physically and spiritually.

In the spring, I read *Surprised by Hope* by N.T. Wright which gave me a new perspective, a hope that one day I would receive a new body in the new heavens and the new earth. Once again, I began to heal with immense peace—physically, emotionally, and spiritually.

I began to embrace life with a profound purpose and the presence of joy. I was still experiencing many hospitalizations, but this new perspective gave me courage, and my faith grew as I kept being reminded that I was made in God's image and that He did indeed have a plan for me. My prayer partner at Gotham often reminded me of Psalm 139:13-14 (ESV): "For you formed my inward parts; you knitted me together in my mother's womb. I praise you, for I am fearfully and wonderfully made. Wonderful are your works; my soul knows it very well."

As I finished my doctorate in New York City in 2016-2017, I applied for a tenure-track professor position in a new city, one where I would be able to do high-impact research at a large public research university. During my last year of study, I moved back home to New Jersey to live in my parents' house to save money on rent and wrote my dissertation in my childhood bedroom. Though I was reminded that I was made in God's image, I had given up on finding love, certain that no man in his right mind would want to marry a girl with a terminal illness. I wanted to move to a new city and start over.

Yet just when I had a little faith, God demonstrated his faithfulness. A close friend joked that I could not leave the NYC area without trying online dating once. She asked me to try it and just go on one date with a Christian man. To appease her, I joined an online dating application and in less than 48 hours, I connected with Daniel, the first Christian guy I "liked" on the app. To my surprise, he is now my husband!

Daniel was different from the others. On our third date, I told him about my illness, sure that the dates would end there. I wanted to be honest and protect myself from any further heartbreak. Instead, Daniel reminded me that I was made in God's image and that the Christian life did not promise us a life of smooth sailing and little suffering. He still wanted to date me, and we became committed to one another within a few weeks.

Having recently experienced the death of his mother, who passed away from breast cancer, Daniel told me he asked himself whether he would want his father to have married his mother knowing that her life would be short-lived. He answered that he would. Daniel's answer touched me.

As we continued talking, I had one more thing to tell him. I was applying for new positions and interviewing for my dream job at NC State University in Raleigh, North Carolina. *Surely now, he would run away.* Yet, he did not. I interviewed for the position and received it. Daniel, in his loving kindness, took a leap of faith and decided to move down with me, but only after we were married. Five months later, he proposed, and I graduated within the same week. Two months after he proposed, we had the most gorgeous wedding, and host the biggest goodbye party for our precious friends and family in NYC and New Jersey.

Moving to Raleigh was a new chapter, and though the year was joyous, my disease made itself known in the background. There was still the uncertainty if I would be able to receive a liver transplant. However, we found out that my chances of obtaining a liver were higher in the Raleigh-Durham area than in NYC. Organ transplantation involves a complicated and lengthy process to get off the wait-list, and NYC was a highly saturated area. The only way to get an organ was to get sick—to the point of death. However, Duke University Hospital offered one of the best chances and outcomes for liver transplantation in the whole nation—and it was only 30 minutes from our home. During our first year of marriage, we went through an intense and emotional process to move my name from the organ transplant list in NYC to one in North Carolina.

In April 2019, I was deep into my second year as an assistant professor at NC State University and feeling stressed. I started developing a strange rash on my leg. I also started having bowel movement issues. Little did I know the two were connected. Prior to my PSC diagnosis, I had also been diagnosed with ulcerative colitis, but I mainly had been maintaining this disease through medication. I had a routine check-up with my GI specialist and mentioned both the irregular bowel movements and the rash to her. She immediately recognized that my immune system was attacking itself in a strange way. The inflammation from the colon was leading to inflammation throughout my body. She ordered a blood test to see if there were any discrepancies. Little did I know that I would not leave the hospital that day. The blood test presented irregularities in my liver enzymes due to the inflammation, and I suffered from another episode of liver dysfunction. This inflammation led me to stay in the hospital for a few days until my liver could function properly again.

The bilirubin level kept rising, leading me to be hospitalized three more times that month. It was a grueling process being in and out of the hospital, and I was told that because of my bilirubin levels, I was considered near the top of the liver transplant list. In fact, I was the seventh (7th) sickest person on the list based on my liver numbers. The nurses told me that there was a possibility that I would get a call that an organ would be available to me. Daniel and I agreed that if I were to ever receive the call, we would go forward with the transplant.

But I had already waited over 10 years for this liver. Could the wait actually be over? I had my doubts. I was finally healthy enough to be discharged from the hospital, and I went home wondering if I would ever receive the call.

On the morning of April 25, 2019, I slept through the most important phone call of my life. Duke Hospital had been trying to call me since 8 AM, but my phone was on silent. My husband's phone rang, and I immediately woke up, it was one of the nurses from the Duke transplant clinic:

"Mr. Lee, we have a liver for your wife. Do you want to accept the organ? You have one hour to get to the hospital."

We looked at each other, remembering our commitment, and said,

"YES!"

We rushed to the hospital, making calls to my parents (who immediately got on a plane from New Jersey to North Carolina) and my colleagues along the way. (Someone had to give a final exam to my students!). When I arrived, I was immediately rushed into the operation prep room, and I heard that the new liver from a deceased donor was already being prepped for surgery. It had all happened so fast. In a matter of hours, my life would completely change. We thanked the Lord for His provision and prayed for guidance upon us. The surgery lasted 10 long hours. By the time my parents arrived at the hospital, I had come out of surgery. The miracle my parents had waited and prayed for had come to pass.

The recovery process was brutal, requiring more than three months to get used to the new organ. Taking a high dose of anti-rejection medications and a cocktail of pills had its side effects, and taking care of my body was a full-time job. Yet just as I was recovering from the surgery and my body was getting used to the medication, my body began to fail, again.

Having a liver disease also meant that I had a very large spleen. My spleen was 4-5 pounds, whereas the average person's spleen is the size of a human fist. The spleen was traumatized after the transplant, and since it was already so large, it could no longer work properly. In June 2019, I was told that the surgeon had to cut my very large Mercedes/Peace Sign-looking incision on my abdomen all over again to take out the spleen.

The spleen, which we affectionately named "Spleeny Todd," had to be evicted. In July 2019, I went through another difficult surgical process, taking another week in the hospital to recover from the surgery. To my surprise, the surgery was even more challenging than the first, as Spleeny Todd had been too large to not touch any of my other organs. The pain was unbearable, and I asked the Lord once again to relieve me from my suffering. As always, He was kind. Slowly, I began to heal and gather my courage. I remembered what Tim Keller said in a sermon when I attended Redeemer back in graduate school,

"True courage is not the absence of fear but the presence of joy."

The Lord is indeed kind and gave me a glimpse of restoration here on earth. He gave me a new body on earth—a new organ—a new chance at life—to live out the calling I had received from Him. Upon reflection of my letter to God in 2015, God blessed me with a career and a husband who when we married knew, that by vowing "in sickness and in health," "in sickness" would be his path. I have seen God's sovereignty in my career, life, community, and especially my health.

Faith is not circumstantial; it is self-forgetfulness. As Ephesians 2:8-10 (ESV) says, "For it is by grace you have been saved, through faith—and this is not from yourselves, it is the gift of God— not by works, so that no one can boast. For we are God's handiwork, created in Christ Jesus to do good works, which God prepared in advance for us to do." This new worldview has given me incredible joy and peace, for we know, as Christians, that every inch of this universe belongs to the King of the universe. Eternal joy is on its way.

Double for My Trouble

My story begins with divorce. Or, to be quite honest, perhaps the infidelity I witnessed at the hands of my father during my childhood.

As a child, I saw firsthand how my father's infidelity and deception plagued his marriage to my mother. The humiliation it caused me changed my opinion of men and dramatically changed how I viewed life.

I experienced an incident as a young office assistant at my elementary school. While on duty, I observed a visit from my father to the school's office. During that visit, my father brought a boy into the office to reinstate him into school, after he had been expelled.

When I saw my father come in, I hid out of sight where I could see and hear him, but he could not see me. He looked a little unkempt, as I'm sure he hadn't been home the night before.

I couldn't hear everything he was saying, but apparently he was unhappy with the behavior of the child, and he made everyone in the office aware of it by his tone and disapproving words. The boy, I assumed, was my father's illegitimate son since he bore the same given name as my father. Wow, what a revelation! Not only did I experience what my children would call second hand embarrassment, I was very disturbed and embarrassed myself. The more I thought about it, the angrier I became. I knew he was unfaithful to my mother because I had experienced other incidents involving his infidelity, so I wasn't surprised that he had other women. An affair was one thing, but another family? How could he have let things go this far?

If this wasn't humiliating enough, my friend, the girl I walked to school with each day, knew my father and his son because they lived right next door to her. So this meant, when I picked her up for school, I had to see my father's car parked in the driveway of his other family's house, the following morning after he had stayed away from home all night.

It happened numerous times and became a joke between my friend and me, but I never actually thought anything was funny about it. I guess you could say I had to laugh to keep from crying. When I would ask my mother why my father hadn't come home on certain nights, she would repeat one ridiculous story after another, about a flat tire, how the car had broken down, or something similar. That still didn't answer the question. Where had he spent the night? I already knew the answer. I never knew whether she knew and was trying to protect me, or she didn't know at all. I didn't tell my siblings until recently, since we have all reached adulthood.

I saw no need to upset their lives the same way mine had been. For one thing, my younger sister, who was the baby of the family, seemed to have a special affinity for our father, which I didn't want to interfere with. Also, I wasn't sure whether my older sister or brother would tell my mother, so I wasn't going to take the chance of having that information possibly break up the whole family.

My mother didn't work outside of the home, so I guess my father at least financially supported us. My father worked the swing shift, so by the time he would get home during the week, I was already in bed. I would be grateful for that in the weeks to come, because that meant I was able to avoid the awkwardness of running into him. However, there is one thing I regret about the entire situation: I never did get to meet my brother. What if there were other children? Years later I tried to find other siblings through social media but never did.

By age 15 I was pregnant, with my first child, by my high school sweetheart. As soon as we graduated high school, we married. Looking back now, I guess our parents were correct when they said at 18 we were too young to get married, but at that age, we were in love, and all we could think was, "What could go wrong?"

We were so happy at first. We built a new house, purchased a new car, and were expecting a baby! We didn't need to schedule date nights because we did everything together. What a joyful time!

My other friends who were also housewives seemed to do nothing but watch soap operas and talk on the phone all day, comparing stories about their husbands and children and cleaning house until it was time to fix dinner. That got old for me after a couple of years, so when I got bored of being at home all day, I went to work for Mutual of Omaha Insurance Company, doing clerical work. By then the other husbands from our friend group began to encourage my husband to go out with them on Friday nights without me. I wasn't bothered in the beginning, since we usually spent so much time together. My husband even took me out to lunch most days. I didn't realize that their boy's nights out sometimes included other women until it was too late. Since they visited nightclubs, there were always women available.

With only six weeks left before our daughter was born, I left work to go on maternity leave. Since my husband and I shared the vehicle we had just purchased, on my first day of leave, I kept the car for the day, to run errands. I dropped him off at work, and since it was a sunny day, I lowered the sun visor in the car while driving. A picture dropped out. The nightmare began!

My husband was seated with a woman on his lap. Based on previous situations, I knew the woman was interested in him. My hormones were already going crazy, so this was the last thing I needed. I was in shock at the sight of this photograph. It was as if I had suffered a traumatic event. The sight of him and her together led me down a path from which I would not soon return. As a young girl, I swore that I would never accept infidelity in any future marriage of my own. I was not going to be my mother, which is why, when it happened to me, I found no road to forgiveness and reconciliation with my husband. I called a friend to talk things out before confronting him. She was all too familiar with cheating, since her husband had an ongoing affair with his childhood sweetheart. I don't know what I was looking for—sympathy, advice, I don't know, but whatever I was hoping for, I didn't get it.

I thought about not picking him up from work and just letting him figure out how to get home by himself, but I picked him up. When we arrived home, I confronted him, showing him the picture and demanding an explanation. Much to my surprise and dismay, he apologized for the photo, insisting it was nothing. To this day, I wish he had just left it at that. Instead, he confessed that he had been having an affair, not with the woman in the picture, but with a different woman. He had lied whenever he said he was visiting his mother's house. I had no idea.

Well, I was not going to end up with a husband like my father, so after many conversations and attempts at reconciliation, I filed for divorce. His mother came to visit me in hopes of facilitating a reconciliation, but her words only made things worse and helped to seal my decision to divorce.

"Your expectations are unrealistic; all men cheat," she said.

Really? If that was what I had to look forward to, no, thank you! I was not going to relive the life I grew up seeing. When she made that statement, I said to myself,

I guess I won't be married then.

(I suppose you could say that it was a self-fulfilling prophesy. I've been married and divorced three times and am still single.)

The sad thing is, I really wanted to forgive him and move on with our marriage. I was pretty naive back then, and although I did not understand why the affair happened, I always believed that he loved me. He confirmed that fact when I saw how distraught he was over the breakup. I came home one day to find him in the garage with the car on and the door shut, hoping to end his life. I probably would have taken him back after seeing his desperation, but my mind would not let me move beyond the traumatic event of the affair.

During the divorce proceedings, my children became legal wards of the State and the court awarded physical custody to my ex-husband because I had moved out of the state to start a new life.

Legal custody was given to the state of Nebraska; we were told they could not place custody outside of their jurisdiction, because of the discrepancies in our testimonies and the multiple accusations we leveled against one another. They determined that neither of us could retain custody on our own civilly, and for this reason, custody was given to the state.

What led to this? A series of events of betrayal between my husband and me. The visitation agreements made between us were constantly broken. On several occasions I would come home from work to find my children gone, taken by their father back to Nebraska, where he lived.

Every time he kidnapped them, I would have to travel to retrieve my children. It happened again and again. Each incident made it more difficult for me to locate my children than the previous one because he continually moved from one city to the next, cities that were all unfamiliar to me.

These occurrences resulted in much anxiety and stress, not only for me but also for my children. I never knew whether I would find my children at home or discover they had been taken away. It was also highly stressful for my children; how could it not be? I remember holding a very disturbing conversation with my son's teacher about an incident that embarrassed him and forced me to make a change.

One day, I arrived home from work, and my children never came home from school. I immediately phoned the school and found out their father had picked them up that day after he had sworn he would not take them again without my consent! This was the last straw! I couldn't take it anymore.

I became so distraught that I borrowed a gun from a friend, which was crazy because I had never even held a gun before, much less fired one.

I left my house around 2 am to drive the 550 miles to my ex-husband's home, not stopping for anything except gas. I arrived around 10 am that morning. It must have been a Saturday since everyone was home. I planned to shoot him and reclaim my children, once and for all.

Those of you reading this are probably wondering how I could think this course of action was the only solution to my problem. But here's the thing. At that point in my life, I wasn't thinking clearly. I was only reacting to the stress and anguish of the situation. I didn't believe I needed to ponder my decision and never considered a different course.

When I arrived at the door of my ex's house, I fully intended to carry out my plan to shoot him. The gun was in my pocket, and so was my hand. But God had a different plan.

I expected my ex-husband to answer the door. Instead, my 10-year-old daughter opened the door. I don't remember what it was about her appearance or expression that shocked me, but I broke down into a tearful frenzy. I suppose that's what jolted me back to my senses. I retreated to my vehicle, determined to resolve the situation a different way.

When I contacted my ex to discuss custody, I fully expected him to be reasonable in the negotiations concerning the children. He had remarried, and I knew that his new wife did not want my children, because she had told me so in the past. She had even poisoned her own children's opinion of me. On a previous visit to their home, her son answered the door, and when I told him who I was, he replied,

"My mom hates you!"

With that in mind, I was hoping he would be willing to restore my children to me with reasonable visitation for himself. But that didn't happen. The only agreement he was willing to make with me was that he would have the children during the school year, and I would have them in the summer.

As much as I wanted my children with me, as I mentioned earlier, my son had already started showing signs of emotional instability at school, I resolved to find a solution that would put an end to the frequent kidnappings.

Even though my ex's behavior would be considered kidnapping today, during the 70's, one parent taking their children across state lines was merely considered visitation. The laws changed significantly during the late 1970's and early 1980's as the courts began to recognize the devastation experienced by the parents and their children.

Back to my story. Even though I agreed to my ex's unreasonable arrangement, I could not emotionally handle the absence of my children from my life. As if this was not enough, my closest friend and even my mother made statements and accusations that caused me to spiral even deeper into despair. My friend implied that I turned my children over to their father, so I could have my freedom. I'd been introduced to drugs by then, eventually addicted to smoking crack. It took my mind away from the emptiness I felt because my children were not with me.

At one point, my mother commented that some women just weren't meant to be mothers. What a stab to my heart. She had no idea how much it hurt me to hear her say something like that. Being a mother was all I wanted to be. It was the fact that I was deprived of it that was destroying my life. She directed me to a scripture in Deuteronomy referencing the curses for disobedience to God.

"Your sons and daughters will be given to another people, while your eyes look on and long for them continually; but there will be nothing you can do," Deuteronomy 28:32 (AMP).

When I read this scripture, I had my ah-hah moment. I knew that I had to make a change to get my children back. The timing of God is perfect and not coincidental. Around this time, I heard a testimony from my sister-in-law, who was married to one of the San Francisco 49ers. She had also been addicted to cocaine and was now free from bondage and serving as the co-pastor of her church. My sister-in-law told me that she had been baptized in the Name of Jesus, filled with the Holy Ghost, and instantly delivered.

She gave me the scripture from Acts 2:38 (KJV) as a reference:

"Then Peter said unto them, Repent, and be baptized every one of you in the name of Jesus Christ for the remission of sins, and ye shall receive the gift of the Holy Ghost."

From that time on, I pondered her testimony in my heart. I began to seek God, in my own way, and He heard and delivered me.

Starting my new life, with God leading me, I was still bothered by the accusations made by my friend and my mother. When I talked to God about it, He led me to the Bible story regarding the wisdom of Solomon in 1 Kings 3:16-28 (ESV).

The story is about two prostitutes who came to King Solomon to have him resolve an argument. The two women lived in the same house and had both given birth to baby boys a few days apart. One of the babies died in the night, and the woman with the dead son took the living child and replaced him with the dead child while the other woman slept. When the mother of the living child awoke to feed him, she knew the dead child was not hers, however, the mother of the dead child insisted that the living child was hers.

King Solomon sent for a sword, and when the sword was brought before him, he said, "Divide the living child in two, and give half to one and half to the other. Then the woman whose son was alive said to the king, because her heart yearned for her son, 'Oh, my lord, give her the living child, and by no means put him to death.' But the other said, 'He shall be neither mine nor yours; divide him.' Then the king answered and said, 'Give the living child to the first woman, and by no means put him to death; she is his mother.'" (1 Kings 3:25-28 ESV).

By guiding me to this story, I believe God was saying to me,

"By what you did, you showed that you were willing to give up your children, rather than have them destroyed in the process of a custody battle, even to your detriment."

My story doesn't end here. Not only was the young daughter I lost in divorce restored to me, but God gave me back double. This daughter is now involved in a jail ministry that God entrusted into my care and ministers alongside me, and He has also given me two more daughters.

"Instead of your [former] shame you will have a double portion; And instead of humiliation your people will shout for joy over their portion. Therefore in their land they will possess double [what they had forfeited]; Everlasting joy will be theirs," (Isaiah 61:7 AMP). **God gave me back double for my trouble!**

A Father's Lasting Lesson

THOSE WHO KNEW MY DAD know that he was his very own kind of special. He loved profoundly but wasn't very warm in his expression of it. He was a merciless teaser and instead of warm embraces, he gave bone crushing hugs and playful punches. That said, if he loved you, you knew it. He loved me, and I knew it. So here comes my birthday. I'm a recently married twenty-something.

We meet at the hospital to welcome my sister's newest addition to her family, baby Matthew. I wait for the greeting and the happy birthday. It doesn't come. I'm shocked and hurt. A few days later it's the weekend, and I'm at my parents' home. My niece and nephew are visiting from the Cayman Islands and, as the designated favorite aunt, I'm there to hang with them for the day. Not one to hold my feelings in, I take every opportunity I get to let my dad know that he saw me on my birthday and didn't even acknowledge that for me it was a special day. As we pass each other around the home, I poke him sharply and scold, "You! You didn't even wish me a happy birthday!" He is busy scaling, gutting, and seasoning fish. He is obviously preparing to have one of his famous outdoor fish fry gatherings.

Nothing strange here. Both our parents are people magnets and had been dubbed Mummy T and Daddy T by all the young people in their church. Having tired a bit of scolding, poking, and prodding my dad for his great offence, I notice the children at loose ends, and I offer to take them to the park nearby. My parents are grateful for the offer, and the children happily skip with me to play for a bit in the outdoors. When they eventually tire, we walk home in time to see some of the usual suspects arriving. As I expected, these are the young folks from the church my parents attend, many of whom are friends I had made while studying at the nearby university.

Suddenly, I see some other friends of mine approaching the gate. They were definitely not among those who were frequent visitors to my parents' home. "What are you guys doing here?" I call out, thrilled to see them, but equally perplexed. By now there is a buzz of people happily chatting and laughing—the usual Daddy T fish fry vibe. "You mean you don't know yet?" my friend Faith asked incredulously, her eyes ricocheting between my face and the already gathered crowd of family and friends. Aba by her side gave a playful chuckle and continued, "DT, this party is for you! It's for your birthday!" I was speechless.

I had witnessed the entire preparation and execution, had even got myself out of the way, so they could carry out the finishing touches, and I had been clueless the whole time. All this had been for me! My dad had not forgotten my birthday, instead he had been preparing to thoroughly delight and surprise me. As you may imagine, I was also very embarrassed. I had chided, prodded, poked, and reprimanded my dad for his grave offence the whole time that he was actively putting in place the surprise of my life.

To boot, he had himself picked out a lovely gift for me —a beautiful chunky necklace and a crafty jewelry box in which to store it. The magnitude of this gesture was not lost on me, because my dad was not known to give special-occasion gifts. As you may imagine, I tried desperately to apologize for my previous remonstrance and mistrust. My dad just smirked and hugged me warmly.

Slow Learner?

FOR MANY YEARS I suffered from sciatica. Even before the children came, the sciatica had forced me to do away with a stick shift and rely on automatic transmission cars. Kingston's rush hour traffic had often caused me to limp home in great pain. By the time the children came and I had undergone multiple surgeries, adhesions became another source of pain. Finally, a doctor in Panama after examining me, felt that most of the pain I suffered all over my body was more than likely due to fibromyalgia.

I had reacted violently to all the classic trigger points. Because of this, I am forced to be gentle with myself. Strenuous exercise, heavy lifting, and the like are things from which, by necessity I am banned. I was not happy, and I complained frequently to my FATHER. After all, HE made me this way.

Why? How mean! "Why didn't I have my children naturally?" All these painful adhesions were making my life unbearable. "Why do I have sciatica?" "Why do I hurt all over?" "Why?" "Why?" "Why?" I poked and prodded my FATHER. I questioned HIS love. I whined. Mid-2017, a friend offered to act as my personal trainer. She was newly certified and positive that she would be able to get me into shape without undue pain. I recounted to her the many previous failed attempts I had endured.

She was not deterred. I said to her, "Let's do this, but know that every time I start a program, something happens to cause me to stop." Our first day began well. We moved through a series of routines walking through our hilly neighborhood, utilizing the new exercise equipment in our park, and finally ending up in my family room for cool down exercises. Everything went so well that I was encouraged. We made a plan to do this three times a week, and I set a date for the next session. Well, as I feared, the next session was not to be. I came down with an awful cold that quickly morphed into a persistent bronchitis.

The next time I saw my trainer, she was peering around my front door thrusting food sent by the ladies of our Bible study group into my hands and refusing to enter my home for fear of catching what I had. I looked at her ruefully and said, "See what I told you? Something always stops my exercise programs." Shaking my head, I retreated to my family room to resume my prone position on the sofa. I had been having sleepless nights filled with violent coughing episodes that sometimes caused me to throw up and grab at my head that at times felt like it would explode. My days, therefore, found me propped up on the sofa trying to grant my body the few hours of the sleep it had been denied. From that position,

I filled my days with YouTube videos. That's when I stumbled upon the interview with War Room lead actress, Priscilla Shirer, our beloved Bible Study writer and teacher. As is the custom with YouTube, the videos skipped from one to the other following the trend of the previous topic. That practice led me to make a discovery. Priscilla Shirer, our favorite Bible Study presenter, was also a talk show host! Who knew! As the videos progressed, she had moved from interviewee to interviewer! Her guest was a slender, middle-aged blonde with a peculiar accent, who spoke with passion about the brain, and, in particular, the concept of neuroplasticity.

Now in full disclosure, the brain and its working were never an interest of mine, but Dr Caroline Leaf, neuroscientist and Christian minister, relayed her information in such a manner that I was riveted. Before I knew it, I was enrolled in "Brain School," as the video stream deserted Priscilla and segued to back-to-back sessions with Dr Leaf. Sadly, I was also extremely weak and breathless. The Bible study group faithfully sent meals to our home, aware that I was too weak to prepare them. I needed to be helped upstairs every night. My many visits to my family doctor and the pulmonologist plus myriad medicines and treatments did very little to alleviate my suffering. I was so ill, I noticed I was beginning to drag my right leg as I walked.

Eventually I concluded I must be allergic to something in my highly treed neighborhood. Jonathan had completed a year of college in Panama and would head out in a few months to complete his studies abroad. Jason was already in the US at college. Jovanna was in her junior year in high school. Selwyn was away on a business trip. So, desperate for relief, I had Jonathan drive me to our home by the beach to spend the weekend. The difference was startling. I felt revived and finally began to breathe and sleep well. When Sunday evening came, I begged to be left there while my family returned to their commitments in the city. They refused to leave me there alone, and worse, without a car.

We agreed that, as soon as Selwyn arrived later in the week, we would return. I returned home, and so did the cough, as soon as we neared my neighborhood. I could not wait for the weekend to arrive. I would retreat to the beach once again for much-needed relief. As Friday finally rolled around, I planned to head straight there. In order to beat the usual horrendous traffic, we would get Jovanna, as soon as school was out at 3p.m. and keep going. Mid-plan, she reminded me that that evening was her school's basketball night. She would need to attend. Not daunted, we decided to make the trip at 9: 00pm when the games ended.

At 9 p.m. I received a call from my husband lamenting the snaking traffic that was still wending its way past the school in the direction of the beach. No worries, we would leave at 11. Surely by then it would be smooth sailing. Already weakened, I climbed into bed planning to get up later for the trip. Both our children decided they were not really keen on going and opted to stay home. Selwyn and I finally decided that, given all the changes and the lateness of the hour, we would ourselves turn in for the night and leave very early in the morning for the beach. That night, Friday the 13th of October, 2017, was the last time I felt fully in control of all my limbs. At 1 a.m. on Saturday October 14, my world, as I had known it, ended.

Life Changes

SOMETIME ABOUT 1 A.M. I attempt to roll out of bed to head to the bathroom. That's when I feel it. There is the distinct sensation of a giant snake wiggling around in my bed. The even stranger thing is that I cannot locate my right arm, as I am attempting to prop myself up. The sensation I feel could best be described as a writhing, frozen, electrical shock. And my right arm is unresponsive.

More precisely, I can't find it. Alarmed, I call for Selwyn to help get me to a standing position. I feel fine except that my right arm, which I can see is there now that the light has been turned on, is totally unresponsive. I make a dash to the standing mirror in our room and begin to do the stroke tests I had often read about: Is my face twisted? No Can I stick my tongue straight out? Yes Do I have a headache? No Can I say my name clearly? Yes Is everything else working? Yes Good! This was not a stroke, I reassured myself. But what was it? In no time Selwyn was dressed and helping me into clothes, so we could head to the ER. Usually when we are needing care at Hospital Nacional, we would first make a call to our family pediatrician Dr Medrano. He would alert whichever specialist we would need to see when we got there. This time, however, that completely escaped our minds. As we rolled up to the door of the ER, and I was whisked inside in a wheelchair, I was filled with confusion.

I was in no pain whatsoever, but my right arm was still not listening to me nor obeying my commands. I quickly got myself registered, and the doctor on call began the preliminary testing. The conclusion was that whatever was the matter seemed to be connected to my nervous system. Coincidentally, the doctor exclaimed, there was a neurosurgeon still in the hospital at that late hour. This was highly unusual, she noted, after she called him to have a look at me. As I lay on the small bed in the ER's brightly lit examining room, I heard voices and saw the privacy screen being pulled open. I was greeted by a pleasant young man, maybe in his late 30's, who first looked at my file then asked if Thompson was my surname.

Though I was on the verge of celebrating my 35th wedding anniversary that December and had long adopted the Batchelor surname, in the Panamanian health system, I am still Diane Thompson. Panama has a system of naming that never discards the maiden name. That practice turned out to be for my benefit. Coincidentally, this kindly young doctor was also a Thompson. And his name, Daniel, happened to be the name of one of my favorite nephews. (In case you're curious, all my nephews are my favorites.) His warm bedside manner combined with our "familial" ties put me at ease.

As he talked soothingly and easily, he was carrying out his own physical examination. When he was through, he suggested I undergo radiographic tests to rule out a stroke, but thought that, given my history, I was more than likely just suffering from a pinched nerve. Selwyn is now convinced that he said that just to put me at ease, for when I suggested that there was then no need to do the brain scan, he insisted it was a necessity.

Given the fact that I was quite lucid, had absolutely no head pain, no slurred speech, had clear vision, I was totally unprepared for what the results revealed. Even as I was engaged in conversation with my congenial doctor, there was blood on my brain. The results confirmed his suspicion that I had experienced the rupture of a blood vessel.

He was able to confirm from the images that it was associated with a very uncommon congenital brain malformation he called an AVM. The results showed an Arteriovenous Malformation. There it was in black, white, and varying shades of grey—I was never completely right in the head! (My children will get a kick out of that one.) The disease usually causes problems such as seizures, headaches, as well as stroke-like symptoms.

I had never experienced any of those. This condition had gone undetected for over 57 years! All these many years later, after an extended period of violent coughing, it had finally ruptured and affected only my right arm. My doctor, whom I soon "adopted" as my brother, marveled that my arm was the only thing affected, given the location of the bleed. Apparently, I could have lost speech, vision, mobility... the list went on. I could have died. I was overwhelmed at the thought. I had been born with this condition. It had been an explosive mine waiting for the inadvertent contact that would have been sure to wreak havoc and even death. This thought became more focused, as Selwyn relayed to me his brother's comment. Selwyn's brother, a surgeon of many years, on hearing of my hemorrhage had exclaimed,

"What a good thing it was that Diane didn't have children naturally!" He had seen not one, but two colleagues die in childbirth, only to realize afterwards that they both had the same malformation as me. Look at GOD! The strangest thing then happened to me. I was being admitted to the semi-intensive care unit of the hospital with blood on my brain and an arm that hung limp, yet I was awash with an inexplicable peace.

I had absolutely no fear of dying. I finally understood what the King James Bible meant in Philippians 4: 7 by "Peace that passeth all understanding." This was amazing. I was not afraid! My first thought was to make sure no one else was alarmed when they heard the news, so I grabbed my cell phone and wrote a quick note making sure that first, they knew I was fine, then that I was in the hospital. Despite that, my friend Flory made it to the hospital that night even before I was transferred from the ER. The next few days were a blur.

I met technicians, sub-specialists and, for the first time in my life, a male nurse. Somehow my bronchitis disappeared in the hospital, and I was finally able to catch up on all the rest I had missed during the previous month. Between my many hours of drug-induced sleep, I seem to have been party to numerous decisions concerning the way forward. I found myself in a sea of words and phrases that made me feel like I had migrated to another planet. "The lesion is near the motor strip. It measures 2.5 cm x 0.7 cm x 0.8 cm. Venous drainage is superficial. This is consistent with a Spetzler Martin grade 2." What did all that mean?

From conversations with my "brother-doctor" I learn that the malformation is too deep in my brain for surgery to be considered. That's because the location of the AVM is very close to the area controlling motor and sensation on my right side. Based on its location, it is considered inoperable. Instead they suggest a process called embolization. "Embolization is filling the nidus with a glue-like substance to occlude the rogue veins." I hope you understood this strange language which, all too quickly, I was being forced to decipher.

Kintsugi

BROKEN POTTERY MENDED with a precious metal. That's what this Japanese word means. I have come to see that GOD has melded HIMSELF into my broken spaces creating a precious masterpiece of HIS own design. I am truly beginning to grasp that my brokenness (my mean times) is my blessing. I get to be the backdrop against which GOD's glory shines. ... we have this precious treasure [the good news about salvation] in [unworthy] earthen vessels [of human frailty], so that the grandeur and surpassing greatness of the power will be [shown to be] from God [His sufficiency] and not from ourselves.

We are pressured in every way [hedged in], but not crushed; perplexed [unsure of finding a way out], but not driven to despair; hunted down and persecuted, but not deserted [to stand alone]; struck down, but never destroyed; always carrying around in the body the dying of Jesus, so that the [resurrection] life of Jesus also may be shown in our body. Therefore, we do not become discouraged [spiritless, disappointed, or afraid]. Though our outer self is [progressively] wasting away, yet our inner self is being [progressively] renewed day by day. For our momentary, light distress [this passing trouble] is producing for us an eternal weight of glory [a fullness] beyond all measure [surpassing all comparisons, a transcendent splendor and an endless blessedness]! So we look not at the things which are seen, but at the things which are unseen; for the things which are visible are temporal [just brief and fleeting], but the things which are invisible are everlasting and imperishable" (2 Corinthians 4: 7-10, 16-18 AMP). "Therefore, I will all the more gladly boast in my weaknesses, so that the power of Christ [may completely enfold me and] may dwell in me" 2 Cor. 12: 9 AMP).

In February, 2019, tests at Johns Hopkins showed that the AVM is reduced in size thanks to the embolization, but it is still there. They feel it has shrunk significantly enough to restore my risk factor to what it was before the bleed. They recommend cyber knife (a radiation treatment) to partially obliterate it. However, after regaining 90% functionality, never having had a seizure nor prolonged headaches, and functioning without medication, I'm hesitant to do further treatment. There's more. They also say that at my "young age" (No laughing allowed!) there is a risk of developing brain cancer from the radiation further down the road. My doctor in Panama, after reviewing my results, agrees with my decision to not do radiation treatment of the malformation. We have agreed to doing periodic six-month, then annual checks to ensure that the malformation isn't growing or developing aneurysms.

I thank GOD for this, and will continue therapy to keep regaining strength and normal function on my right side. I am beginning to realize that, before I was born GOD had tucked a love note into my brain. It was one of those "Do not open till..." It was in the form of an AVM. Through this malformation I have come to grasp the depth of my FATHER's love for me that no perfect day has ever been able to convey.

Through it I am being propelled further into purpose ¾ HIS purpose for me. I also thank GOD that through this hard experience in my life (this mean time), I have come to embrace a group of fellow travelers who all suffer from brain AVMs as well as AVMs in other parts of the body. We have become the family we never knew we had. We grieve with each other and we rejoice with each other. Like my 21-year old self at the concert tightly gripping Janet's hand, we hold each other up, as we step onto the world's stage. We know we are not alone. We wait in hope."

Excerpted from *GOD IN THE MEANTIME: A Story of Trusting God's Voice and Embracing His Timing* by Diane Batchelor

What Time Is It? Timing Versus Time

"My steps are now slower, but as I look at my life
Oh, the joy I have known
And my heart continues to hold onto past memories
That help me to keep on keeping on!"~Denise Sutton

Time is defined as "the indefinite continued progress of existence and events in the past, present, and future regarded as a whole. Timing is defined as the choice, judgment, or control of when something should be done." (Oxford Languages, 2024)

What has puzzled man through the ages is how much control we have over time yet how little control we have over timing. The second revelation angers, confuses, and weakens us, causing us to feel helpless at our most vulnerable moments. So, if God gives us control over our time, why does He not do the same with the timing of things in our lives?

In several passages in the KJV Bible, Jesus stressed that "my time is not yet come" (John 2:4 and John 7:6). The verses of Matthew 24:36-42 elaborated that no one knows the time of God's return. So why is timing treated differently than the time we have control over? The answer is that timing is everything. Only an All-Knowing, Omnipresent God knows when the timing is best suited to help complete His overall plan for creation.

So, what is a promise? According to the dictionary, it is a declaration or assurance that one will do a specific thing or that a particular thing will happen. So, a promise offers hope but may also hold a stipulation we must abide by, for it to occur.

When asked to participate in this project, I jumped at the chance to join something that would affect future generations! I wanted to be clear about the project's objectives to make sure that my input would coincide with the Visionary Force behind it. I began looking up the definitions of hope, (which is a feeling or expectation that something will happen), and resilience, (which is the capacity to recover quickly from difficulties).

I will say that I concurred with and understood the meaning of all these definitions. Since I am to discuss my resilience from despair, what better way to begin than to start from what initiated some of my pain? Despair holds many meanings, but I can sum up its power as anything that knocks the wind of hope from your body, spirit, and soul. I have experienced much despair in my family, most horrifically by the deaths of my closest family members.

I will never forget that late night call in 1993 from a hospital with news that changed the future of our whole family dynamic. My sister answered and after a few seconds passed, we heard a piercing cry:

"My baby! My baby!"

Let me back up a little. Earlier that morning, her daughter, who lived in New Jersey at the time, had called to tell us that she had fallen down some stairs and had broken her hip. She would need surgery to correct it. After we learned that her operation had started, our family, who lived in North Carolina, waited anxiously by the phone. Around 10:30 pm that night, we received the phone call... Hearing the instant cry of pain and unbelief from my sister told us all we needed to know: my twenty-six-year-old niece was no longer with us. She had just entered a whole new world (death), and the rest of the family had entered one too.

Life would throw many more grievous surprises my way. A second event that tested my resilience was my father's failing health in 2001. His heart had weakened to the point that it stopped during dialysis and the doctors had to restart his heart through a shock treatment. Doctors gave us the following choices concerning his care: continue the shock treatments to revive him during dialysis, or to perform heart surgery to possibly strengthen his heart. The family decided "no" to both as we knew the shock treatment was too painful to justify its purpose and that his chance of surviving heart surgery was minimal.

Our remaining choice was to make him as comfortable as possible as the toxins built up in his body. We knew that eventually his body would no longer be able to sustain itself.

He would then be allowed to peacefully transition, and that is what he did.

My father's death added to my despair, and as the number of dying loved ones increased, the empty spaces filled my heart with dark clouds of heaviness. Yet, the weight did not end there. I also witnessed others go through similar tragedies, searching desperately for ways to cope and not fall apart. Their pain touched me and magnified my sorrows.

The advantage of experiencing similar situations as others do, whether before or after them, is that you grow in empathy, knowing first-hand what they are feeling. If your experience comes after theirs, you can see that survival is possible and by learning the skills needed to get past the trauma. Over the years, I have learned that my strongest support to others has often been to lend a listening ear, allowing the person to find their own coping mechanisms as I had to.

"Bad timing" can bring on weighted feelings. And our loss of control forces us to trust God, our All Powerful Being even when we don't quite understand all the details.

I am learning more to trust God's timing in everything I do, so I can handle the despair that may come without letting it overwhelm me. Instead, I will choose to grasp hold of God's promise for me.

After my father's death in 2001, Mom's resilience showed through. She adjusted by becoming more active in community, church, and family functions. I knew a major reason she was able to do so was that she could now concentrate her efforts more on herself and my youngest brother, who was nine years older than me but had the mind of a five-year-old. My mother often worried about who would take care of him if something happened to her first. She felt even with good intentions, others would eventually see his care as a burden. Therefore, I think she secretly spoke to God on this matter. I'll tell you why in a bit.

I had moved back home around 1989 while pregnant with my daughter. I eventually graduated from nursing school and began working in mental health. Not wanting to give up on my love and passion for writing, I constantly wrote articles, books, songs, and anything else that allowed me to spread my words to the world. I continued to expand my efforts, publishing several books, producing music, and recording in the studio. Mom believed in me from the start and elected herself as my number-one fan.

Both of my brothers also lived with us, but the one who was mentally challenged had an innocence about him that brightened our days. One habit made me uncomfortable, though, was that he would run up to me, kiss me on the cheek, and say unexpectedly, "I love you". I guess you could define him as being an affectionate person. I was uncomfortable with the gesture and often wished he would stop, often turning from or pushing him away when he attempted it. The problem was not that he was inappropriate, but that public affection was not easily expressed or shown in our family.

I would often do things with my brother and remember returning home from an out-of-town trip one Sunday. The date was October 11, 2009, during Goldsboro's annual fair. I felt an urge to take my brother there and let him ride the go-carts that he loved so much. But procrastination hit hard that day, and I opted out, since I was tired after returning from my trip. I promised him a raincheck. I felt a little bad knowing he had been home and was probably waiting all weekend for my return so that he could go. He did not make a fuss about it, but I could feel his disappointment as he said,

"Okay,"

and walked away. I eased my guilt by telling myself,

There's always tomorrow...

The next day, I went to spend time with and support my sister, who was sitting with her husband in the ICU. This trip was an hour and 15 minutes from where we stayed, so there was no other family with her at the time. I was there a couple of hours when my mom called. She told me to come pick up my brother because the site in his arm for his dialysis had clotted.

The medical team needed to put a temporary shunt in his chest until they could reopen the one in the arm. It would need to heal before they could start using it again. Her call necessitated my traveling to meet her and my two brothers halfway between our home and the hospital.

I called my daughter, who was attending the community college nearby, and asked her to drive the three of them so they could transfer into the car with me, and I'd drive back to the hospital I just left in Wilmington. When we met, I asked my older brother to take over driving, and I moved to the back seat with my brother, who was about to go into surgery. There was no apprehension about this surgery because he had undergone this simple procedure many times before.

Fortunately, he was not experiencing pain, was familiar with this type of surgery, and showed no concerns or worry.

Thinking back now, if I had realized at the time how fragile life is, that ride with him would have been different. We would have talked about the toy cars he loved so much, his day at dialysis, or some of the things he would do later in the day after surgery or tomorrow.

But I did not pay attention to any of these things and remained engrossed in texting and surfing the internet on my phone.

My brother recognized he did not have my full attention, so he spent his time listening to the radio and conversing with my mom.

Arriving at the hospital, we knew the routine; we'd been through it so many times before. They called my brother back to pre-op. The family was allowed to go back with him while they prepped him for surgery. I told my older brother and mom to go without me because I was still tired from traveling.

My mother and older brother came out after a few minutes and the three of us were escorted to the surgical waiting room, where the family had a second chance to go back and visit. Again, I turned down the invite, encouraging my older brother and mother to go alone while I waited until everything was over.

As they came out, my older brother was smiling and was carrying my younger brother's clothes and phone, saying,

"Larry gave me his Michael Jackson shirt and told me to take care of it."

We all laughed at that. We would definitely not let anything happen to his MJ shirt!

I was hoping the surgery wouldn't be long, for I was torn between being with mom or my sister who was still with her husband in ICU, at the same hospital, on the same floor, but several hallways away. My sister knew I had gone to pick up our family to bring my brother to surgery.

The three of us waited as the procedure began and progressed. My younger brother's phone rang a couple of times during the operation, but I didn't answer it. Who would be calling him? It couldn't be that important!

We all knew the drill. After surgery, the family would be called to the post operative conference room so the doctor could talk to us about the surgery, postoperative procedures, and plans for replacing the shunt in my brother's arm for dialysis as the chest was a fragile place to keep the catheter. In its present location, it was prone to infection.

We walked in expecting to hear all the instructions that, by now, we knew from memory. But as the doctor began to speak, the conversation was different. There was no small talk. The doctor spoke so rapidly, I know he crammed all his thoughts into one sentence by quickly saying,

"I'm sorry. Something happened when we pulled out the catheter in his chest. His veins were weak. We tried everything we could, but we lost him on the table."

The doctor looked at us, waiting quietly for what he said to sink in. My mind went into delayed reaction mode as I stood there still listening for the "He did well" part and "We'll begin using his arm shunt soon," but I didn't hear that because, for some reason, he didn't say it…. As comprehension of what he had just said began to sink in, I felt the weight of darkness begin to cloud my surroundings as I again was entering into a new world with one less loved one to talk to. This was it. The end. Without warning.

This time, my older brother reacted more quickly than even my mother.

"No, no, not my riding partner!"

The two of them often went places together. My mother stood there crying,

"My baby. My baby."

To overcome my helplessness, I analyzed everything by becoming the "rational" thinker.

Did this man just tell me he killed my brother on the table? How am I going to tell my sister in ICU, who was preparing herself to say goodbye to her dying husband, that she had just unexpectedly lost her brother?

With death, especially a sudden one, grief is never the first reaction. There is a time frame where your senses have to catch up to reality. What "was" becomes a dream world as you face what "is" now standing before you. And that numb denial takes over as a coping mechanism. This transitional state allows you to function as you go through the motions of what to do next.

So many things ran through my mind of what I would have done differently in the last few hours: I would have talked to him all the way to the hospital while we sat in the back seat. I would have visited with him both times it was offered to the family to go back and see him. I would have taken him to that fair yesterday. And as the nurse of the family, I would have asked that doctor to wait and do the surgery the next morning when he was probably not tired from doing other surgeries.

I then turned my anger towards the One I knew could have changed the situation in a way that neither the doctor nor I could have.

God, I'm angry now. You knew Your timing for my brother. Why didn't You tell me some way to do something different?

I knew God had given me several chances to do those things I did not do, but I didn't take them, so when I heard no response, I could not say anything else.

We did get a chance to see my brother, but we had to see him lying there with the tubes from his throat to his back that they had used to try to drain the blood to keep it from filling up his lungs. I demanded the staff to remove all the tubing so this would not be our last viewing of him at the hospital. But they insisted they could not remove anything until an investigation was done, so we left my brother there with that picture of him forever embedded in our minds.

Yes, I did walk through the hospital crying, in shock, to tell my sister, and we cried all the way back to the waiting room, where my older brother and mother were. My sister eventually went back to be with her husband, who needed her presence more.

While driving home, my mom admitted to my older brother and me that she suspected something because earlier in the day, when my younger brother was waiting for his van to take him to dialysis, he jumped up from his seat, ran and kissed my mom on the cheek and said, "I love you!" which he doesn't normally do while waiting intently for his van.

I knew my mom had already had that secret talk with God because she somehow knew.

I knew it! I knew it! I knew it! I know she asked God,

"Don't let me leave him down here for someone else to care for."

After his death, everyone in the family began adopting my younger brother's openness in showing affection and saying, "I love you," without skipping a beat. Now my younger brother's care was no longer an issue.

Around two years later, Mom went for a follow-up appointment after the doctor saw an x-ray of her left lung that looked suspicious. I'll never forget the day I took her to the doctor, and she tried to talk me out of going inside. The previous year, six months after my brother's death, she was diagnosed with and successfully fought breast cancer with radiation and surgery. This year, she did not want to "fix" anything else.

"Let me live and die in my time,"

she'd say.

"Not an option,"

I would answer,

"You're not leaving me."

The irony is that I struggled to pull her out of the car and make her start the process over again to ensure she'd be with me a long time, but that did not happen. She suffered more intensely with this next round of treatment because she had chemotherapy, and she did not respond well. And, because she was going through a second round of radiation in the same area as her breast cancer, her esophagus was burned. It hurt her to swallow food and liquids. She eventually died less than two years after starting her lung treatment. Two factors which worked against her were her age and her reaction to chemotherapy.

At first, my brother's unexpected death consumed me, but in later years, my mother's death became the harder battle to fight within because of all the things we had shared and the ways in which she had supported me over the years.

I grew really angry after her death, but knowing I couldn't ethically harm myself and face God, I did the next closest thing. I stopped doing things that were healthy, waiting for all my health issues to do what they do best and eventually "take me out," so I could be with my family members who left me without checking with me first.

Over the years, I have learned not to focus on my pain but to use it to help others with theirs. I realized that each of my experiences has helped me to empathize and understand how others in similar situations might be feeling. A loss from years ago can be just as painful as one that happened yesterday if there is no closure. When talking with someone going through tragedy, whatever the cause, sometimes listening can be the best remedy because, not knowing the dynamics of a person's relationship with the deceased, you cannot compare situations and may not always give advice that they want to hear or will help them. It feels good to encourage someone by saying, "I know what you are going through."

These are some of the things that helped me to cope. Being able to rise after the fall and help someone else get up has been the one shining factor of surviving tragedy. As the years go by, I feel more thankful and understanding of how God's timing doesn't have to match mine to work the miracles I have seen.

I still have my moments of being in awe of the fragility of life, even my own, and of certain days or events triggering my grief. I have grown from learning about those things that normally would have made me weaker. What helps me? Observing how others handle their tragedies, seeking advice from those who I feel know what I am going through, studying and meditating on the Word, and constantly praying and listening for His answers to my concerns. I trust God's timing completely, not understanding everything but knowing confidently that I don't need to see the end of God's plan for it to work in my life and in the lives of others.

My mom encouraged me years ago to write a poem with the title, "Keep On Keeping On." She was so proud of it and would often push me to quote it to others who would come to visit us. Years later, after her death, I see the silent message she left for me to keep moving forward even though she is not here with me. I often quote it to remember never to stop!

"Keep On Keeping On" by Denise Sutton (Inspired by Mrs. Willie M. Sutton)

"So give up? No way! Throw in the towel, not today.
Because of the goodness God has shown,
I know I'll receive an even greater reward
If I can just keep on keeping on!"

An Excellent Partner

The child of God's faith journey is shaped in resemblance to His greatness and perfection. Far from our human grasp and comprehension, His unfathomable plans and strategies inadvertently shape us into His masterpieces of wisdom and careful individualized caring . ~Carolina Alford

I was born into a traditional middle-class family in South America. This story about a Protestant family spans over half a century. They live within a traditionally Catholic cultural environment.

James was a humble and duty-driven attorney, brought up in poverty and honor while enduring his father's alcohol misuse.

He married Mary, a highborn bride, the first-born daughter of an educated military general and a strong rural woman, radical in her beliefs. Mary became the honorable secretary to the president of their country's central bank. Her determined and stoic personality would prepare her for the difficult road of her heroic life.

Five years of courtship turned into marriage and produced a large family, two stillborn children and three living daughters. James and Mary remained committed to each other and their new family.

James was a dedicated provider, Mary was a visionary and outgoing homemaker. Both were devoted to their three beautiful daughters, Celia, Marsha and me. For some years they enjoyed the blessings of family life.

Then the hardship started.

At age 14, the oldest daughter, Celia, a great looking and gifted girl, began experiencing debilitating neurological symptoms that required the most progressive and qualified neurologists to explore. Heartbroken and confused, my parents looked for every avenue to afford expensive trial treatments as they continued supporting their young family.

Appalled and challenged by the household's painful heartbreaking reality and very conscious of the daily pain that consumed my parents, Marsha, the middle child, became the responsible daughter. An honors student from K-12th grade. Marsha focused on being all her older sister could not. Her motto was:

"Be part of the solution, not part of the problem."

She continued to consistently excel at everything.

Celia's health grew progressively worse. Her bodily functions declined, leading the family on a journey of financial drainage. My parents, Marsha, and I continued to navigate each day as a family in tragedy. However, we relentlessly strived for the whole family's well-being, in this 'new normal'.

Eventually, Celia became involved in a relationship with a youth at risk from a local school, introduced by a maternal aunt.

This youth was a troubled person with absentee parents and was raised by his elderly grandparents.

Against the families' preferences, the young couple eloped and got married. They eventually depended on my parents' support for their two baby daughters.

Celia's health continued deteriorating, and my parents continued caring for their own children and the two grandchildren. By the time the grandchildren, Pauline and Carine, were toddlers, their father was an alcoholic, unable to find employment, and frequently mistreated Celia. In addition, he had sexually molested his oldest daughter. As a result, he was expelled from the family household.

While my parents fulfilled their responsibilities despite depression and anxiety, including being caregivers for the two grandchildren, Marsha persisted in her academic performance despite the collective pain and her powerlessness to change the fate of our family.

As the youngest child, I was trying to survive. I was in an environment I couldn't decipher or adequately perform in. My outgoing personality attracted the attention of my peers, some of whom I chose against my better judgement.

As the days passed, I soon faced the reality of becoming role model to the loud, rambunctious and disturbed children of my sick sister. Our family system was under constant stress.

By age 14, I started experiencing conflicted feelings in connection with my faith.

Where was the help and support from the God that my family had worshipped for a long time?

Why was the oldest daughter sick with such a strange and incapacitating disease? Why had her delinquent husband assaulted his own children? Why was this family forbidden the opportunity to live a normal life like my friends and classmates who would not even self-proclaim as Christian believers?

Despite my extended maternal family's tradition to hosting many American missionaries, and faithfully serving the Christian church as a family for decades, my family was not enjoying the fruit of a blessed life.

I eventually considered this "God" to be a scam and figured that life would be better without the burden of His mandates and the fake 'spiritual' lives without joy or practical hope.

My family's life soon worsened. The animosity, verbal altercations, door slamming, anguished cries, arguments among the three younger ones, and substance use became a constant in the home. The only times these episodes would abate were when Celia's new health trials would send her into a deeper and darker health-related abyss, and our attention was turned to her while we drowned in a combination of guilt and despair.

Not long after this, I became involved in several consecutive self-destructive relationships. Although I had other options, I foolishly chose a popular, ambitious, and outgoing man who was very unattractive but a great leader. Spending time with this man would eventually be the first of several bad decisions.

I stopped fellowshipping with the community of faith, further experimented with drugs and alcohol, failed at multiple attempts for professional stability as an organizational social scientist, and married someone who not only led me to further substance use, but who also exploited me financially and emotionally. Hughes (the influential leader mentioned earlier), also led me into deceiving and stealing from others, including my family and our common friends, and using financial schemes.

After three failed pregnancies, 11 years of misery, repeated infidelity, and Machiavellian ruses, we divorced.

Celia, now fully confined to a wheelchair and unable to talk, experienced chronic swallowing and breathing problems. She required around-the-clock care. To further complicate matters, my parents' health started declining due to diabetes and chronic kidney failure.

Pauline and Carine carried on their young lives while navigating the shame and hopelessness of having a sexually abusive father and watching as their terminally ill mother became sicker.

They were labeled as youth at risk during their teen years. There seemed to be no promising life ahead.

I spent years in a life of promiscuity and personal, relational, and professional failures.

Staggering under frequent illegal substance misuse, one day I encountered a former older female client of my father's who had connections with a different type of faith community than the one I grew up in as a child.

Ginny and I immediately bonded. She introduced me to a Bible institute that challenged the traditional religious style I had known. I enrolled in studies, and within a month of attending experienced a transformation in my life.

For the first time, I saw myself as someone who could live her faith practically, a way in which I could have a relationship with a real God and walk by faith according to the words He had spoken, not a prefabricated religious system full of guilt and prejudice.

The final finding of meaning and purpose in life were finally here! I became actively involved with the Bible institute, where I experienced the fullness of joy by receiving the mysterious and controversial baptism in the Holy Ghost with the evidence of speaking in tongues. Whenever I would pray, pictures of people I was divinely interceding for appeared in my mind. Much spiritual growth and progress were evident as I continued in the church and Bible institute. Opportunities for volunteering, serving in the helping ministry, and actively reaching out to others with the love of Jesus abounded. Amid the passionate love for the lost that Jesus died for, and while involved in the ministry, I was asked to lead Bible studies focused on the nation of Israel and lessons the church could learn from their devoted observance to His Word and Principles of Life. After all, they wrote the Torah and sacred scrolls about the eternal God, and Jesus was Jewish, and also a Rabbi.

The study group drew the attendance of Ghora, an immigrant Russian nuclear physicist, an iconographic artist initially dedicated to painting and restoring centenary artwork of the highest level according to the Russian Orthodox liturgical tradition. He was deeply involved with the crème of Russian and Romanian diplomats in my South American city. I was convinced that this exiled member of the Romanoff Russian aristocratic family was a present to me sent by God.

Ghora faithfully attended the church and Bible institute with me. I had already assumed many responsibilities as class monitor, worship singer, and leadership staff. Yet I took it upon myself to support this incredibly handsome man's expressed need for Christian spiritual companionship. Not only that, but there were also frequent financial favors, because as he put it,

"The life of an immigrant starting iconographer is hard in a new country."

Not long after, Ghora delved into relationships with a multitude of women from different churches, single women like me, wanting companionship and owned sizable bank accounts. As though this was not heartbreaking enough, I inexplicably lost the eyesight in my left eye.

The final blow came two days later, when I received a diagnosis with the same illness as my sister Celia. The disease that had laid the final stroke to Celia's life after 30 years of debilitation was now attacking my body, yielding a dark and hopeless prospect of dying crippled and fully dependent on others. *Was it my turn now? Was I to follow her in the devastating steps of this incurable and terminal disease?* I was only thirty-six years old.

In spite of this tragedy, I was blessed by my newfound church. The leaders made immediate arrangements for me to attend a spiritual retreat at a Christian healing school so I could be under the ministry of God and His Word all day long since there was no medical cure for my illness. To my anguish during my spiritual retreat, Ghora got involved with some of my Christian sisters.

Upon my return from the spiritual retreat, I found that I had not only lost my boyfriend to one of my church sisters, but had also lost my job at the central bank while I was fighting for my life. However, during the retreat and involvement with the ministerial site, I met many wonderful Christian believers. Sister Juanita, a humble and most generous Chicana elder was my host at her own home. Juanita opened her house and family as a haven of faith and comfort for me. She offered a safe refuge with the hope that God had a plan and future for me.

During the intensive and long Bible studies and health ministries offered by the Healing School staff, I met many seasoned Christian believers, instructors, and students from all around the world. One of them was a Louisiana born man, ordained for the work of the ministry by a world-renowned preacher. Warren was an army veteran who had served in Germany. We dated for three years and decided to get married. My health was stable with a miraculous stagnation of all symptoms and total absence of relapses.

Warren and I happily started our lives away from my family troubles and from Warren's birth family, who were scattered around the country. We both became employed at a lively church. As the days passed, Warren struggled to hold a stable church life, was challenged at maintaining gainful employment, and could not take care of himself.

I was a full-time worker and a full-time housewife. So, after much trying for yet another 11 year marriage, unfortunate instability, lack of emotional intimacy, and further decline in financial, and spiritual growth, I left the home and relocated to start a new career in mental health.

Shortly afterward, my body broke down. I lost eyesight in both eyes and experienced some of the same challenges as my sister Celia during the early stages of her illness. However, I thanked

God for the support of my immediate family, spiritual family, and employer. After all these years, I am grateful as I remember my sister, and my employer who relocated me. My employer provided all my moving expenses, and completely furnished my new office and new home.

I spent several weeks in prayer, self-examination, restitution, and meditation of the Word of God. By His grace, my physical relapse subsided, and I returned to normal life, able to drive and live independently once again.

As a mental health provider, I found opportunities at community-based organizations, non-profits and public employment. So much was happening during this season; I discovered a new congregation that delved into the fullness of the Biblical canon and the Jewish roots of Christianity. Life was very good.

Eventually I found a job working with at-risk youth. While at that job, I received an email inviting me to interview for a position with a much-desired United States program. What was this? God had heard my cry, and I received the best invitation of my life! God, in His faithfulness, opened the door to another job! I would become a mental health clinician in a field that was new to me but would utilize my almost 20 years of experience working with local children and families.

Following this latest blessing, I was asked by a neighborhood friend to attend a Christian coffee house. I attended a few times. There, I was approached by the manager; a good looking, retired, single, baby boomer. He had a Christian background, significant property and financial assets in the rural area. He was well known in the community. We dated for six years, after which I left him because of worrying personality traits, spiritual lukewarmness, and a history of alcohol misuse. I left but not without first serving and ministering to him the love of God and His compassion though the many health challenges and happy days that we shared.

During my life, I have traveled a twisted and cumbersome path, just as the path traveled by the nation of Israel: 40 years of twists and turns instead of the 11 short days of walking. My path has been one that God carefully and lovingly has guided me through; like a persistent thin thread of Jesus's red blood lovingly following me to protect my safe passage to reunite with my Heavenly Father. He Who from the beginning had already assigned Holy Spirit to stay by my side every step of the way.

My life has been full of sad and happy adventures, convincing me that my most excellent walk-along partner is He, Who has never left or forsaken me.

After decades of savoring the fruit of God's faithfulness, compassionate rescues, and Fatherly outreach, I hope all who read this story will come to recognize the fruit produced by the Eternal God of the Universe. My prayer is for you to see the fruit in my life, and desire God to produce the same in yours.

When the Church Stays Silent—the Noise of the World Grows Louder

"I'm sick and tired of being sick and tired."
— Fannie Lou Hamer

So finely ground into our daily lives is the "American" history of the founders of this country, along with their extraordinary efforts and deeds, that to dare mention racism or the value of humans of all skin hues has been made to seem impolite—rude, even. Why would I bother to bring it up?

Because 2020 left a jagged scar across my church life. And I was tired. Soul tired. Fannie Lou Hammer tired. Her words resonated from the depths of my heart.

Ahmad Aubrey—shot and killed as he innocently jogged through a neighborhood one February day in 2020, Breonna Taylor—gunned down as she slept in her bed one fatal night in March 2020, and George Floyd—killed in front of helpless and horrified onlookers in May 2020.

And my majority-population church was silent, as were so many other churches, whether they were majority-population or mildly integrated.

During the summer of 2020,

the community CALLED,

the city SCREAMED,

the state SHOUTED,

and finally,

the nation ROARED,

and my church was silent.

I began to experience a range of emotions quashed in many previous years. The silence amplified a feeling I knew but hadn't felt in a long time—marginalization. The silence—not, for example, a moment of revered silence or prayerful acknowledgment, but quietly ignoring what was happening in the state and country, as if it was okay. It was not.

Ignoring issues of race sent the message that the experiences, struggles, and concerns of race were not valued or worthy of discussion or, again, prayerful consideration. When sermons ignored the racial tension and issues of the day, I could feel myself disconnecting from my faith community as I attempted to find consonance between my spiritual beliefs and my social and cultural realities. Ignoring issues of race during sermons or public prayers often made me feel dismissed or invalidated. Didn't my concerns warrant attention (Was it intentional)?

I grew increasingly frustrated when we as a body failed to address the systemic injustices and inequalities we were all witnessing either through media or a simple drive through downtown. The number of senseless shootings in the Black and Brown communities and the overarching issues of race were deeply personal and deeply painful, not because I knew the victims, but because the victims could just as quickly have been one of my relatives. But was I surprised, or did I feel betrayed by sermons cleansed of racial connotations? No, sadly, I was not.

Why do injustice and mercy, when spoken of in conjunction with race, receive only a cursory nod from churches? Why are there no moments of silent acknowledgment? Why no sermon series that look deeply into healing the wounds of God's people? We are all wounded. Tragedies of such a national scale leave us so, no matter our skin tone. When did this kind of silence become acceptable to Christ's followers?

The silence of the church on racial and social injustice is a complex and troubling phenomenon that stems from a variety of factors, both historical and contemporary. As I contemplated the leadership's silence, most troublesome was the palpable fear that demanded that the church stay silent—the fear of causing division within the congregation. Discussions about race and social injustice would indeed be uncomfortable and possibly lead to disagreements among members with different perspectives.

Still, such conversations could ultimately lead to healing, deliverance, and forgiveness. However, when church leaders chose to avoid these topics altogether to maintain a sense of unity within the congregation, it was grievous because, at best, it was a false sense of unity.

For some members of the church, particularly those who benefit from systems of privilege, perhaps it was simply more comfortable to ignore or downplay issues of racial and social injustice. Confronting these issues may have required them to acknowledge their complicity or make sacrifices to advocate for justice.

Several within my church invited me into difficult and hard conversations; they were troubled by the silence but, as far as I could tell, never broached the subject with leaders. Some members sought me out more from a sense of "Christian duty," and others pursued me from a genuine empathy and desire to understand what was happening in the culture and with me as an individual.

In all fairness, I met weekly with one of the pastors who initially invited me into a conversation to show his willingness to listen to and learn from those most affected by injustice. He did a few check-ins with me, and sometimes I left the talks wondering if I was heard.

The underestimation of the realities of discrimination and the attitude that if we don't talk about it, it will go away created even more of a burden of invisibility for me. Despair became a heavy burden, both physically and emotionally. Internally, I grappled with feelings of surmounting sadness. I often thought about this scripture:

"This is what the Lord Almighty said: 'Administer true justice; show mercy and compassion to one another.'" Zechariah 7:9 (NIV)

I get it; churches may interpret their faith in ways that prioritize individual salvation over societal transformation. This theological perspective may lead them to focus more on personal piety and spiritual matters while neglecting social justice and equity issues. Additionally, specific interpretations of scripture may be used to justify maintaining the status quo rather than challenging systems of oppression.

In that case, where will this scripture fit? "To do what is right and just is more acceptable to the Lord than sacrifice." Proverbs 21:3 (NIV)

But if the choice to remain silent in light of all that was happening around us made *me* feel marginalized or ignored, wasn't it also harmful to the other people in the congregation?

Addressing the church's silence on racial and social injustice required a concerted effort to confront these underlying factors and foster a culture of openness, humility, and solidarity within my congregation.

I felt caught in a relentless battle, and despair overwhelmed me. I remember feeling trapped in a cycle of negativity, unable to envision something different for my church. Even reaching out for help felt like an insurmountable hurdle. Many of my friends within their congregations felt much the same way. One friend K. called me and said she needed an intervention; she was one of a handful of Black women at her church, and although the pastor was not African American and taught fairly open messages on racial reconciliation, the issues dividing her congregation were crushing.

Three of us went to her rescue and spent a few hours praying and listening to her talk.

After leaving her home, I decided that only prayer could help me survive my own despair. I spent the next few days in prayer. Was I to remain in an all-White church, the one to which I knew I had been called? Was my time of service finished? I heard these words in my spirit:

"Season of Lament."

I was vaguely familiar with the concept of lament, but I began to search the scriptures diligently for a more perfect understanding. The Lord was instructing me to step away and spend my time of soul-weary grief and mourning with Him. I wrote to my pastor and ministry leaders immediately.

My heart is heavy at this writing,

> *I am being called into a deep season of lament for our church, our city, and our nation. I am not angry but grieving. I am not upset but wholly peaceful. I am seeking the Lord with all of my heart. During this time away, I fully expect God will prevail as He always does and bring His people to a place of Kingdom fulfillment, not just speaking 'love to everyone' but living it.*

> *I solicit your prayers and your support as I step away from ministry. If by chance you find you have questions or concerns about any of my current responsibilities or obligations, please feel free to contact me directly. If I may ask yet another favor, please do not forward this letter to anyone. This is not a matter of discussion for the church, but a matter of prayer for you as a leader if you choose to pray for me.*

God bless you as you carry on in His service.

In truth, making this decision tended to make me sadder, and I made that known. I mourned over this for several days and cried unto the Lord about what to do. I was not leaving the church; I was still a member. However, I discovered two things that gave me clarity.

The first was based on a quote from Walter Bruggeman, an Old Testament scholar. He asked a question:

"What happens when lament is missing from the life of the church?" The answer?

"When you lose lament, you lose the sense of justice because lament is the crying out against injustice. I think it's also crying out for justice in the face of injustice. Our nation is in trouble because of racial issues, and our church should not be."

Lament is an important Biblical value. Lament is usually not spoken of in the sermons as a series in many of our Western churches; it is not often heard in our songs. Preaching and singing about suffering, grief, and pain are less attractive than blessings, prosperity, and joy.

Through Biblical lament, God would help me confront and process my emotions and experiences in a way that honored Him, while at the same time using prayer to pinpoint injustice and become a catalyst for change. Perhaps I would motivate a culture of compassion and empathy within some members of my congregation, if not all.

Stepping into the process of lament became somewhat easy. Although it meant stepping away from ministry and social interactions with friends, we were in the middle of the pandemic, and most of us were staying at home anyway. Ceasing engagement with social media, movies, and television did not present a challenge either. I wanted the peace of God, and I was willing to do whatever needed to be done to have it.

Lament is a powerful expression of grief, sorrow, and mourning. It transcends mere sadness; it is a deeply emotional response to suffering, injustice, or loss; it acknowledges the reality of pain and suffering in the world. There is an intensely sacred dimension to lament; we no longer have to suppress what we feel but release our plea or cry for help directly to God, and to God, I cried out. Daily.

Lament also means bringing those feelings of despair, anguish, and pain to God, He already knows, but it is a time to be honest as we pray from deep within our souls. So, when life is disrupted in a way that we do not want it to remain, or we are experiencing the feeling of powerlessness in our suffering, we may cry out, "God, if you do not act, we are without hope." Yet we also know that nothing is beyond the hand of God. Lament ultimately led me to an intimacy with God I otherwise would not have known, but for my season of lament.

So, for the next three months or so, I committed to walking in transparency with God and others in times of sorrow and despair rather than smiling and pretending all was well, acting as though we had it all together. No one does anyway, at least not all the time.

The second point of clarity or revelation concerns something exciting the Holy Spirit did to confirm this season of lament—Satan tried to conduct several interviews with me, calling into question whether or not I'd heard from God.

"God wouldn't tell you to leave the ministry; this is all your idea, blah blah, blah."

One day, I woke up in the wee hours of the morning. The Holy Spirit told me to look at the time, which I did; it was 4:17 am. I groaned and was just about to turn over when He said, write down the time, which I did; then He said,

"Turn to the scripture."

I was a little groggy and not following what was going on, so

He said,

"You've been studying the book of Lamentations; turn to the scripture."

Here's what I read:

"Moreover, our eyes failed, looking in vain for help; from our towers we watched for a nation that could not save us." Lamentations 4:17 (NIV)

Does this scripture sound like it could be a news headline? It is not the nation but the church where effective help and salvation will ever be found. That was pretty much all the confirmation I needed. The Lord awakened me several mornings, thankfully not all in a row, and I soon learned to check the time on the clock, find the scripture, and pray the prayer prompted by the words I read.

He was building my resilience. Engaging in lament was starting to help me build resilience in the face of adversity. By writing down and confronting my pain and distress head-on, I developed the emotional strength and fortitude to look more deeply into the problematic circumstances of race and division at my church.

God would faithfully teach and show me scripture to overcome challenges. What's more, He would show me how to navigate grievous situations and conversations surrounding deep-seated racism.

My purpose in crying out and seeking God for heart change at my church was so we could all arrive at a place of Shalom.

As I studied the myriad laments found throughout the Bible, particularly the Psalms, I also studied other writings from pastors and theologians who understood the principles of lament and dared to teach them.

Here is a quote from one of my favorite teachers, Soong-Chan Rah. He was a pastor and now teaches at North Park Theological Seminary. A few years ago, he wrote a book titled *Prophetic Lament*. His book provides a biblical and theological lens for examining the church's relationship with a suffering world. Speaking at a conference he said,

"Lament is a reminder of a God who is able to do more than we've allowed Him to do because we have only seen God in our celebration and victories, so lament reminds us that God is present not only in the triumphs of our day-to-day life, but also in the suffering of our day-to-day life."

I love this particular quote because often people think that if you talk about injustice or suffering, it is not glorifying God, not Christian, or it makes them uncomfortable. They want you to change the subject. My response swung from shutting down to pursuing the topic anyway.

If nothing more, lament will produce a healthier outlook and a more profound spiritual connection between us and Heaven and those here on Earth. As the days passed, I witnessed this metamorphosis within my heart.

My purpose in crying out and seeking God for heart change at my church was in the hope of bringing attention not to myself but to the injustice of racial inequality, the suffering it causes, and the need for racial reconciliation and healing. If my season of lament inspired or encouraged others to mobilize and my faith community to advocate for a more just and equitable society, Praise God. If that result was not immediately recognized, Praise God.

His purpose would be accomplished one way or the other; my only job was to be obedient to what He asked of me.

I had no goals or aspirations when I first began lamenting. As God took me deeper into His Word and His presence, my heart's desire blossomed into a picture of what life in a healthy (not only mine) faith community looks like; I wondered if we would, if we could, all arrive at a place of Shalom no matter how we thought, believed, or most importantly, looked.

When the Lord made it clear that He was ending my season of lament, I recognized that through the acknowledgment of my pain and soul tiredness, healing was happening. By giving voice to my pain and sorrow, emotional restoration seemed to flow in me. God understood. God saw. God helped me to reclaim my agency.

The LIGHT would always outshine the darkness.

What else came out of this period away from ministry and alone time with God? Words formed in my heart, and I wrote; the experience was cathartic as I penned essays, music, and poems that became a poetry collection.

Tears flow from our prayers,
repentance bows our head.
Our ears are dulled to cries for mercy.
We've winked at injustice,
turned our face from truth
and wrongly ignored strife.
Our souls' weariness becomes
the goad by which we now come
with sins piled higher than our heads.
We lift our hands yet higher to receive
that which we've often withheld:
forgiveness, grace and peace.
Let now our lament fill the heavens.

~MFW

My return to ministry and church has somehow fostered some measure of solidarity and empathy within my faith community.

As I've shared my journey of lament, it has begun to create a sense of connection, a much more supportive, albeit not perfect, environment for healing and change. Along with my story of the season of lament, I close with this poem, also written during my time away.

Psalm 139:14

Ochre, amber, ebony, sepia earth tones for earth skin:
I am fearfully and wonderfully made.
Long, short, kinky, curly hair for wonder's sake:
I am fearfully and wonderfully made.
Straight, flat, wide nose for freedom's fragrance:
I am fearfully and wonderfully made.
Thick, round, full, thin lips for words of hope:
I am fearfully and wonderfully made.
Big, piercing, gentle, curious eyes for searching out truth:
I am fearfully and wonderfully made.
Fisted, open, praying, reaching hands for grasping grace:
I am fearfully and wonderfully made.
Walking, running, protesting, standing on strong legs for justice:
I am fearfully and wonderfully made.
Beaten, broken bodies surviving for greater things:
I am fearfully and wonderfully made.
Gifted, challenged, curious, inspired minds set for eternity:
We are fearfully and wonderfully made.

~MFW

Author's Bios

Crystal Chen Lee is an associate professor of English education at North Carolina State University in Raleigh, NC. Her research lies at the nexus of teacher education, literacy, community engagement, and underserved youth, especially youth from immigrant and refugee backgrounds. Crystal is the founder and director of The Literacy and Community Initiative, a university-community partnership that amplifies youth voices through student publication, advocacy, and leadership. She was a high school ELA teacher in New Jersey and received her Ed.D. from Teachers College, Columbia University. Crystal is a child of immigrant parents from Taiwan and attends Holy Trinity Anglican Church in Raleigh, NC.

Clydelle Winfree

As a young girl growing up in Omaha, Nebraska, Clydelle loved to spend the summers with her grandmother, who took her to church regularly; however, she began her walk with the Lord as an adult at the age of 34. She is the mother of 4 adult children: Brian, Monica (Adewale), Gabrielle (James), and Michaela. She has nine grandchildren and 10 great-grandchildren; and is a very active presence in their lives. She is a real estate and mortgage professional with a Bachelor's degree in paralegal studies and has recently completed a four-year law degree program with Northwestern California University. As an Elder at the House of Joy Miracle Deliverance Church, she is a teacher, preacher, intercessor, and legal adviser who oversees the Women's Department and heads up the Jail Ministry. She loves to travel and spend time with her family, but she says what she desires most is for God to get the glory from her life and to hear Him say, "Well done thy good and faithful servant; enter into the Joy of the Lord!"

Diane Batchelor

Diane is a former language educator and shipping industry executive. Born and raised in Jamaica, she has made Panama her home since 2006. She is co-founder of Hibiscus Moms, a Jamaican family support group. Diane sings and ministers with the Christian music group, New Creation Generation International. Diane is the author of the book, *God in the Meantime,* a story of trusting God's voice and His timing.

From her many years of facilitating women's Bible studies, Diane has developed a heart for 'ladies in waiting.' As a survivor of a ruptured arteriovenous malformation (AVM), her desire is to help those seeking God's intervention in their painful life moments to not lose hope while they wait. She is married to Selwyn, her university sweetheart, and is mom to three adult children.

Carolina Alford

Carolina was born into a traditional middle-class family in South America. She relocated to the States as a young adult, but her family remains overseas. She cherishes her community of faith. Carolina walks, and listens to podcasts regularly. She is a mental health provider and volunteers with her city police department. Carolina loves animals, especially her little dog. She also loves people and enjoys spending time with the elders in her life. Carolina likes to travel and hopes to do more in the near future.

Denise Sutton

As a small-town writer with over 25 years of experience, Denise's inspiration stems from the rich tapestry of her family and community. Denise is a nurse, author, songwriter, and poet. Through her company, *My Words and Me*, Denise specializes in spreading inspirational and educational messages through books, social media postings, readings of her poetry, and performances of her songs. Her mission is to encourage others to adopt words as your own that will empower you!

She began professionally writing in 2003. She has three poetry books: *My Words and Me, Do You Know Him?* and *In It To Win It*, and one inspirational book, *Seizing Opportunities That Propel You Forward.* She was also the chief editor and writer in a collaborative book for Sarah's Refuge Domestic Violence Organization, entitled *Breaking the Silence: Victim No More.* In 2005, she collaborated with singers within her community to produce a full-length CD of songs she had written. Since then she has written numerous other songs found on YouTube. Denise communicates actively on social media.

Mari Fitz-Wynn

Mari Fitz-Wynn is a nonfiction author, novelist, and Bible teacher. Mari spends much of her time nurturing the spiritual well-being of communities worldwide as a teacher and trainer for healing prayer ministry. Her ministry has carried her across the globe. She is the author of *Take Heart: 26 Steps to a Healthy Home Schoo*l, *Connect the D.O.T.S.*, a poetry collection, *RISE UP: Poems of Protest Poems of Praise*. She has contributed to several anthologies, including *Connect Faith, The Timing of Everything Promised, Vol. I*, and *Poetry Ink*. Her work has been published in several women's ministry magazines. Most recently her poem *Play Basie, Play* was recently published in *Jerry Jazz Musician* magazine. Mari is a 2018 United Arts Professional Development Literary Grant recipient and a member of the prestigious Redbud Writers Guild. She was inducted into the archives of the N.C. Museum of History as a *She Changed History* candidate. In 2022, she founded Faith Journey Publishing, a long-time goal and heartfelt mission to empower Christian BIPOC women who are forty-five and wiser to write their stories.

Vina Mogg

Vina Bermudez Mogg loves to create with words, paint and paper from her porch on the waters of the Puget Sound. Her experiences as a mother of four, caregiver, and now as Lola (Grandmother in Tagalog) inspire stories that reflect God's restorative love in her devotionals and book projects. If you don't see her in her Adirondack on the porch with a cup of coffee and her cat Louie, find her on Instagram @vinabmogg or online at <u>vinabermudezmogg.com</u>